The Discovery of the Five Great Lakes

Also from Westphalia Press
westphaliapress.org

- The Idea of the Digital University
- Masonic Tombstones and Masonic Secrets
- Eight Decades in Syria
- Avant-Garde Politician
- L'Enfant and the Freemasons
- Baronial Bedrooms
- Conflicts in Health Policy
- Material History and Ritual Objects
- Paddle Your Own Canoe
- Opportunity and Horatio Alger
- Careers in the Face of Challenge
- Bookplates of the Kings
- Collecting American Presidential Autographs
- Misunderstood Children
- Original Cables from the Pearl Harbor Attack
- Social Satire and the Modern Novel
- The Amenities of Book Collecting
- The Genius of Freemasonry
- A Definitive Commentary on Bookplates
- James Martineau and Rebuilding Theology
- No Bird Lacks Feathers
- The Young Vigilantes
- The Man Who Killed President Garfield
- Anti-Masonry and the Murder of Morgan
- Understanding Art
- Homeopathy
- Ancient Masonic Mysteries
- Collecting Old Books
- The Boy Chums Cruising in Florida Waters
- The Thomas Starr King Dispute
- Ivanhoe Masonic Quartettes
- Lariats and Lassos
- Mr. Garfield of Ohio
- The Wisdom of Thomas Starr King
- The French Foreign Legion
- War in Syria
- Naturism Comes to the United States
- New Sources on Women and Freemasonry
- Designing, Adapting, Strategizing in Online Education
- Gunboat and Gun-runner
- Meeting Minutes of Naval Lodge No. 4 F.A.A.M

The Discovery of the Five Great Lakes

by Sara Stafford

WESTPHALIA PRESS
An imprint of Policy Studies Organization

The Discovery of the Five Great Lakes
All Rights Reserved © 2014 by Policy Studies Organization

Westphalia Press
An imprint of Policy Studies Organization
1527 New Hampshire Ave., NW
Washington, D.C. 20036
info@ipsonet.org

ISBN-13: 978-1-63391-113-0
ISBN-10: 1633911136

Cover design by Taillefer Long at Illuminated Stories:
www.illuminatedstories.com

Daniel Gutierrez-Sandoval, Executive Director
PSO and Westphalia Press

Rahima Schwenkbeck, Director of Media and Marketing
PSO and Westphalia Press

Updated material and comments on this edition
can be found at the Westphalia Press website:
www.westphaliapress.org

The Discovery *of the* Five Great Lakes

BY

Sara Stafford

DEDICATED
TO
My Mother

Port Arthur Harbor

Lake Superior

ROYAL Superior—greatest—best—
　　Boundless, nigh, from the East to West;
"Hidden Sea" is the name it flaunts—
Deeper than mystery's deepest haunts;
Ever its billows are rolling o'er
Priceless treasure—a kingly store;
Ever its ceaseless undertow
Summer winds from the meadows blow,
Searching each grove and caverned wall,
Spruces, like sentinels, guard it all.
Beautiful, now, in the noonday sun;
More so, still, when the day is done,
And the shafts, that proclaim the night,
Draw from its breast, the colors bright; ,
Ever its bosom undulates,
Ever on to the tortuous straights,
Sirenlike is its moaning tide;
Tomb of all who have come—and died;
Merciless, cruel, yet grand, sublime,
Thus will it flow till the end of time;
　　.　　.　　.　　.　　.　　.　　.　　.

Would that Nicolet might, once more,
Come from the past to thy smiling shore,
Or, Dulhut see thy troubled brow,
Ah, that thy sponsors might see thee now!

The Sleeping Giant

The Giant's Foot

Discovery of the Five Great Lakes

How Nanna-Bijou Made the Five Great Lakes

WHEN Nanna-Bijou was a little boy there came to his father's wigwam an old medicine man, who built a conjuring tent near his home. Nanna-Bijou was filled with curiosity to see and do the things the old conjurer was doing. One day the old man said to Nanna-Bijou, if you will bring me the silver fox skin that is fastened on your father's wigwam, I will give you five little green stones, and you will be able to turn yourself into anything you wish to be, by dropping one of them at a time into running water. Now the conjurer had made Nanna-Bijou believe that the voices he heard in the tent were the green stones talking, and Nanna-Bijou believed him. Near his father's wigwam was a large forest, and Nanna-Bijou had many times watched the rabbits playing through the wood, and he thought he would like to be a rabbit. That evening he brought the silver fox skin to the old conjurer, who immediately handed him a moose-skin bag with the five green stones in it. The next day he went in the wood where a small stream ran into the lake. There he threw a green stone into the water, and was im-

Discovery of the Five Great Lakes

mediately turned into a rabbit. The landscape was familiar, and after playing in the woods he found himself near his father's home. Here he played for a time, but it was not long before he began to wish that he was a wolf. The wolves at first thought he would not be able to keep up with them, but it was not long before he ran so fast he could take side trips and be back on the trail waiting for the pack. On one of these side trips he met the God of Water, and became so fascinated with his actions, that he would watch him for hours. The God of Water did not like this, and became angry at Nanna-Bijou for following him so closely. One morning Nanna-Bijou changed himself into a black stump and lay upon the shore, where the God of Water came to bathe, and not seeing the stump he stubbed his toe against it, and becoming angry, he kicked the stump several times. This made Nanna-Bijou angry, and when the God of Water came out he struck and wounded him in the side. Then the God of Water leaped upon Nanna-Bijou and tried to drown him. The clouds seemed to burst like a thunderbolt from the sky, and the gurgling of the waters and the roar of the waves bewildered Nanna-Bijou, and a panic seized him. Fleeing from his enemy, he felt the waves grasp the back of his head and deluge him. Suddenly his right arm was powerless, then a feeling like hot lead ran through his bosom, then his right leg had no feeling and his left leg was partially disabled; surely his right foot was gone and now his left, leaving only a portion of his left side and arm free. Seeing a tall cedar tree rising out of the water, he climbed into its branches, and as the animals were swimming for their lives, he saved many of them by pulling them into the tree with himself. As the water rose higher and higher, Nanna-Bijou commanded the tree to

Discovery of the Five Great Lakes

grow. After a time the water began to recede, and for seven days he waited, then he sent down a muskrat to see how deep the water was, but the muskrat came up dead. Then he sent a beaver, who came up with a bit of earth in its paw. Nanna-Bijou broke some twigs from the cedar tree and planted them, when instantly there came up trees and shrubs, making islands and woods. Then he started around to look these islands over, and to his horror found that his right eye had become an island. Afterwards it became known as Michipicoten Island, and his nose became Michipicoten Harbor. The back of his head was a large body of water, one of the largest lakes, with an entrance to the other lakes at Sault Ste. Marie Canal. He called it the "Hidden Sea," because he could not see it, but later it was called "Lake Superior." His right arm became Lake Michigan and his right leg Lake Huron, after the frowsy-haired Hurons. His left leg became Georgian Bay, while his right foot was named Lake Erie, and his left foot became Lake Ontario. Still angry at the God of Water, Nanna-Bijou came up to Port Arthur, and here, wading out nineteen miles, he became tired and lay down to sleep. On awakening he found he had formed the Thunder Cape, with the trees growing out of his mouth and chin, and has ever since been called "The Sleeping Giant." Then Nanna-Bijou began to feel lonely, and thought he would go and find his people, and having one green stone left, of which he made Isle Royale. His adventures will be told in my next chapter.

Discovery of the Five Great Lakes

The Mystic Names of the C.N.R.

The Indian names of the C.N.R.,
Famed for their music both near and far,
The essence of rhythming and tone so sweet,
Charming to senses of all they meet.
Ojibway hunters, preceding us long,
Left their fame in this jingling song:
Of names we find wherever we go,—
Never we'll realize the debt that we owe.
There's Great Kakabeka, like a strand of the dawn,
Meaning, "More waters are following on,"
And River Mokomon, a beautiful name,
Fitted indeed to that river of fame;
Then Mattawan Junction, a hamlet obscure,
Blessed with a name 'twill forever endure;
Mabella, Sha-Qua-Qua the prospect affords,
Taking their names from two Indian lords.
Then Keego-fish and Crawfish Lake,
Next on the line that the travellers take.
Then Abwin is nigh—a place truly blest,
As shown in its name, with quiet and rest;
And Windigo next, a nickname that's famed,
For Windigoostigan, as the Indians named.
Kawene is next, and though it means "Nay,"
Belies its cognomen in many a way.
Then Rowan next, a word of the Gael,
That holds in its breast a remarkable tale,
Of men of the mines, who came years before,
And prospecting there, found a valuable ore.
The name "Hematite" you surely will find,
Familiar to all who have roughed it and mined.
'Tis thus we go on to the end of the rail,
Each name sings a song and tells us a tale,
A story of villages bounteously blessed
With all of the riches of East and of West.

Discovery
of the
Five Great
Lakes

Lake Huron

JOSEPH LE CARON came to Canada in sixteen hundred and fifteen, with four Brothers of the Recollet Order of Franciscan Monks. Champlain had invited him to come for, he said, the Indians were living like brute beasts without religion or God. The four Friars were ready to brave all dangers, and immediately they came they set to work. Le Caron had been given the West; he was the most enthusiastic of the four. It was the season when the Hurons and Ottawas came to the Beaver market at the Island of Montreal. Le Caron could hardly wait to begin his work, and when he first saw the Indians in their canoes laden to the water's edge with bales of furs, he could scarcely believe his eyes. When meeting the savages his heart went right out to them, and he said I will give my life for the good of these men. He wore a long gray robe of the Recollet Order, with a knotted cord around his waist. His head was covered by a peaked hood, which was turned back to protect his bare, shaven crown. On his feet were only sandals strapped about his ankles. He carried no firearms, and displayed no authority. He was so different

Discovery of the Five Great Lakes

from other men that the Indians were filled with awe when they looked at him. They thought he must be a higher type of being, and hearing that he did not want to buy furs, but wanted to live with them and do kind acts, they were astonished. The Chiefs invited him to go home with them, and he said, gladly will I do so, for I am your brother, and I will spend the winter in your villages. Champlain sent twelve soldiers as a bodyguard to this important expedition into the Huron country. Only a few of them knew how to handle firearms. Even the Friar had to paddle his own canoe and help on the way. Soon they were in the country of the Nipissings, who were reported to be sorcerers and spell-makers. The Algonquins said they were not to be trusted. They hurried on for fear of the Nipissings, thinking they would cast a spell upon them. Then they had to stop and get food, for they had eaten up everything. They ate roots and shot birds and squirrels on their way. The canoes would glide for miles, while the shores had long stretches of land on either side. It was July, and the sun poured down on the poor Friar's head. At times he would fall back, and his friends would take him in their arms and bathe his brow. They were going along when suddenly he heard loud cries from some of the boats, and raising his head he saw a vast sea stretched until it met the blue sky in the distance—to the right and left and southward as far as his eyes could reach. Then he rose suddenly to his feet, he has forgotten that he is a Friar, and that his whole mission is to carry the Cross and convert these savages. He can scarcely wait for his canoe to reach the mouth of the stream, and shooting out into the struggling waters beyond, he dashed his hands into the water and, raising it to his lips, he cried the water is sweet, there is

Discovery of the Five Great Lakes

no taste of salt in it, nor anything bitter; this does not belong to the ocean, this is the life-given Mer Douce. This is the great fresh water sea that the Indians have told us about. Here landing, he sank on his knees and, holding the Cross high to Heaven, he thanks God for bringing him safe to this place in the wilderness. His heart is beating with joy at the discovery; then he remembers his mission is not to explore new lands, but to bring souls to Christ. The conversion of one single soul is more important than the discovery of a million seas. Here he kneels at the foot of the Cross and dedicates his life anew to that great purpose. It was in July, 1615, that the first of the five great lakes was discovered by the French. It was called the "Mer Douce," or "Fresh Water Sea"; by the Hurons later it was called Lake Iroquois, but that soon gave way to the first title Lake Huron, so keeping the memory of the frowsy-haired Hurons who lived on these shores.

Dawson Road

Hudson Bay Money now Extinct

Discovery of the Five Great Lakes

Lake Ontario

THE Huron warriors were getting ready to go on the war-path; they were feasting and rejoicing, for they had been victorious in a great many battles, and meeting Champlain and his men as they were journeying through the country, the Frenchmen were anxious for the Indians to go on, but the Indians kept up their feasting and dancing day after day, and did not seem to care whether they went on the war-path or not. When ready, about twenty-five hundred swarthy warriors started for the Iroquois country. They sang and danced and seemed full of hope, but after three days' journeying near the Iroquois country, they heard of a nation who were friendly to the Hurons, who were called Andastes. Their village was near the head of the great river, and they could muster a thousand warriors if necessary. They had always sided with the Hurons against other foes, and they promised to aid them again. The Hurons were

Discovery of the Five Great Lakes

wondering how they could get word to them about the great war party that was now gathering. There was not a doubt but they would send their young men to help fight the Iroquois, so they held a Council, and twelve warriors, who were chosen with all haste, were sent by the most secret route to the village of the Andastes, to get their promise to fight. Champlain thought it would be wise to send one of his white men along with these warriors, and he had no trouble making his choice, for he knew Etienne Brule was just the one to send on this dangerous errand. You can see on the map the course of the great war party of the Hurons on Lake Simcoe, which bound their country on the south. A flotilla of canoes were awaiting them, and embarking in these, they paddled eastward along the northern shore for about twenty miles. Then carrying their canoes through the woods for a long way, they reached a chain of smaller lakes and streams that formed the headwaters of the river Trent. They made many stops on the way, feasting at each friendly village and fishing in the beautiful streams, hunting the deer and small game in the dense forest. Late in summer the canoes suddenly glided out from the mouth of the Trent, and Champlain's eyes sparkled at the sight of the great water expanse which he had heard of from his Indian friends. Lake Ontario was now the second of the great lakes to be beheld by the eyes of a white man. Etienne Brule had probably passed this lake on his way to the village of the Andastes, as he paddled his canoe several days before, and the honor lies on both Brule and Champlain.

Graveyard at Silver Islet

This lonely path and graveyard rough,
Lies at Silver Islet upon a bluff.

Discovery of the Five Great Lakes

The Discovery of Lake Erie

THE last of the five great inland seas to open her secrets to the world was Lake Erie, and the honor of its discovery fell to Joliet, the son of a waggon-maker in Quebec. From early boyhood Joliet had been educated by the Jesuit Fathers for the priesthood, and expected himself to become a priest. When he reached the age of twenty-four years, Talon, the Intendant of Canada, hearing of the great hidden treasure of copper ore concealed in the lake regions, was so filled with ambition to discover where it lay, that he immediately journeyed to France and laid his plans before Colbert, the Prime Minister. By all means, said Colbert, discover its deposits and find some way to send it to France. If this is true, it is more important than if you found out a new route to China. When he returned he heard of Joliet, that he was a young man of rare good sense, cautious and brave in time of danger, and he entrusted him with the task of exploring the shores of the upper lakes, and discover, if possible, the great hidden treasure. Joliet chose a young friend named Père as companion, as he had spent a great part of his time on the rivers and lakes, and knew something of the Western wilderness. This was in sixteen hundred and sixty-eight, when the two young men set out without definite idea how long or where they were going to stay. They spent the summer of sixteen hundred and sixty-nine on the shores of Lake Superior, but found very little copper ore. From the Indian tribes they heard of a great water to the east and south, but could obtain no definite information. Joliet was anxious to explore, but Père advised a postponement until the next year. They turned and retraced their steps to the outlet of the lake. They passed the Sault Ste. Marie, where was a Jesuit Mission. Passing the rocky Islet of Mackinac, they saw Lake Michigan stretching her waters as far as the eye could reach. Here they came upon a band of Indians, the Winnebagoes, and smoked the peace pipe with them, and hearing many stories of a great water further east. They did not stay long at Green Bay, but pushed their way through unknown waters, going through Lake Huron until the lake narrowed down to a strait, now known as the St. Clair River. Following this quiet stream, they came to a lake expansion known by the same name as the river, and entered the broad channel of the Detroit River and Lake Erie, being the first white men to discover the last of the five great lakes fifty-four years after Father Le Caron first gazed in wonder and delight at the Mer Douce of the Hurons, and thirty-five years after Jean Nicolet passed the Straits of Mackinac and paddled his canoe on Lake Michigan. Joliet, if he did not find much copper, added to the world's knowledge of Canada, and his discovery of this wonderful inland sea has had great influence upon the present developments of the Dominion.

Discovery of the Five Great Lakes

Georgian Bay

THROUGH the beautiful islands of the Georgian Bay are left many signs of the fierce battles between the Hurons and Iroquois. Wishing to live peaceable lives they retired to the Manitoulin Islands and the Christian Islands in the Georgian Bay. The Manitoulin Islands are teeming with romance and story of the wars between the different tribes.

Discovery of the Five Great Lakes

Detroit

THE most famous of all the commandants who from time to time had charge of the Post at Mackinac was a French Captain named La Motte Cadillac, and it was he who first saw the importance of a fort or settlement on the Strait de 'troit, between Lake Huron and Lake Erie. This strait, he said, was the key to the Upper Lakes and the fur-producing regions around them. It was through this strait that the Iroquois sent great parties to the rich hunting grounds of the North. It was through this strait that the English east of the Alleghanies had been trying secretly to open trade with the Indians of the Upper Lakes. If a strong fort is built on this shore, both the English and the Iroquois would be held in check. La Motte's plans were received with favor by the French Colonial Minister and he was commissioned to carry them into effect. On one of the last days in July, in the first year of the new century, he took possession of the site where now stands the city of Detroit. He had with him fifty soldiers and fifty traders and workmen, besides two priests, one a Recollet Friar, to minister to the troops; the other a Jesuit Father, to preach to the Indians. They built the fort close to the water's edge, with a stockade of wooden pickets and a small blockhouse at each corner. Within this enclosure several houses made of logs, and thatched with grass, were soon ready for the officers and soldiers. La Motte called his fortress Fort Pontchartrain, in honor of the Colonial Minister, but it was known as Fort Detroit. Then the Indians began to build villages above and below the fort, looking to La Motte Cadillac for protection against the Iroquois. The Hurons from Mackinac, the Miames from the western shore of Lake Michigan, and the Ottawas at Mackinac, secretly sent La Motte a necklace as a sign that they would come when they had gathered their harvest. They all lived in dread of their powerful foe, the Iroquois. Cadillac advised them to weep over their dead and let them sleep coldly until the day of vengeance should come, and he would help sweep away their enemies, which he did.

Discovery of the Five Great Lakes

Daniel Greysolon Duluth

WHO was Daniel Greysolon Duluth? He was a cousin of Tontys, a friend of La Salle, and one of the most adventurous Coureur de bois of his time. In the autumn of 1679 he first visited the country of the Sioux west of Lake Superior, not far from where the city stands that bears his name. The fur traders of Montreal claimed that either Frontenac or La Salle had sent him there to buy furs contrary to the law or agreement which had been given to the Monopoly of Canada, of trade in that region.

Duluth

Proud Duluth, of commerce king,
Greetings from the world I bring
To thy unseen soul; lay at thy feet
Commands to build, grand and complete.

Blessings to thee, for thou hast found
Fertile earth and glowing ground,
Granite ledge and silver mines
And wide stretch of pointed pines.

Thy massive boulders strewn in air,
Naught to these treasures can compare.
Duluth—Superior, hail to thee,
Twice-crowned king and doorway to the sea.

The Dawson Road in Summertime

Fort William Harbor

Discovery of the Five Great Lakes

Mackinac

High on the crest of the Mackinac
Stands the Court of the Pagan Law,
Where, for the love of the martyred Christ,
Priests went forth to be sacrificed;
Hallowed spot, where the night winds bear
Prayers of the martyrs who suffered there—
Tales of the Governor Cadillac,
Fiend, incarnate, whose torture rack
Crunched the bones of the holy men,
Testing their faith as it ne'er had been!
Thus 'tis Mackinac stands to-day,
Towering, glowering o'er the Bay—
O'er the spot where the Indian braves
Tossed their tithe to the greedy waves;
Here, where Ojibway clans of yore
Met by the waters that lapped the shore,
Seeking through cavern and dell and nook
Whistling breezes of Tabihook.
Now but a gull soars high o'erhead—
White-winged thoughts of a past that's dead;
Here, in the darkness, the whispering breeze
Is but the sighing of Iskooshes,
God of the Air, as the Indians hold—
Pagan god of their fathers of old.
Nightly he, and his kindred there,
Dance to the cadence of Pukwas, fair,
O'er the Turtle (aye, they've a mind,
Mackinac's shaped of the Turtle kind).
Close at the head of Michigan's tide
Flashes a beacon—a mellow guide—
Pointing a path for one to advance
Leading him onward to A-Wau-Chance,
Place where the scion of Michibu
Met and was greeted by Manitou.
Here, at sunrise, trying to reach
"Arch Rock," sentinel of Mackinac Beach,
Manitou's guest climbed clumsily,
Dashing the rocks and the earthwork free,
Tumbling it down with a careless grace,
Forming "Manitou's Landing Place."
Here the visitor chose to bide
Deep in a cave on the other side;
Upward, over, the highlands sweep,
Crowned by the fabled "Lovers' Leap."

Discovery of the Five Great Lakes

Legend says, and the tale is told,
How a maid, in the days of old,
Sirenlike, called her swarthy love
Up to the crags and the peaks above;
Held a tryst with the warrior there,
Then, in a frenzy of love's despair,
Dragged him down to the depths, 'tis said—
There they found them embraced—and dead.
Now the breezes, that croon and sigh
Through the beeches and cedars nigh,
Bear the tale of the love-lorn maid,
Tell of her love and the price she paid.
Years ago, before white man's oars
Paddled a course by these inland shores,
Came a sailor—a Cavalier—
Seeking trade and adventure here—
Robert La Salle, and his hardy crew,
Steering the "Griffon" to waters new;
Here they revelled in sailors' rout,
Found a cargo, and put about,
Heading their vessel towards Erie's shore—
Sailed to the East to be seen no more;
No one knows where their craft was cast—
Buried now in the mystic past.
Here was fashioned and put afloat,
"Walk in the Water," a magic boat,
Heedless, alike, of the oars or wind,
Marvellous, quite, to the Indian's mind:
Banners, three, have been flaunted o'er
Mackinac Straits and the flanking shore—
Banners, three, have the wind gods tossed,
Blood of heroes the price it cost.
First came France with her valiant men,
And nailed her flag to the staff again;
Then the cross of the Royal George
Spread its folds o'er hill and gorge;
Then the banner of Freedom smiled
O'er the crags and the peaks so wild.
Fate then labored and bore a man.
Man of all—in whose veins there ran
Blood of heroes, the gallant Clark.
Hist'ry pictures a midnight dark,
Paints the American fleet, so frail,
Stealing on 'neath its shortened sail,
Under the mouth of the scowling port,
Under the eyes of the strengthened Fort.

Discovery of the Five Great Lakes

Lo, when the sun arose from rest,
Casting its shafts to the jewelled West—
Blazing a path like a golden road—
Flag of Freedom and Union glowed!
Over it, ever, a spell is cast,
Whispering tales of the mystic past,—
Dreams of the times that the years enfold,
Living still in the legends told.
Hark you well, when the sunset dies,
Then it is that Keewaden's cries,
Low, like a mass for the yestermorn,
Are, on the wings of the northwind, borne.
Cross the grey of the coming night
Waw-Waw, the Wild Goose, wends her flight,
Guided, perhaps, in her air trail by
Ishkoodah, comet, who roams the sky
Ceaselessly—ever—both near and far,
Drawing his light from the evening star.

. . . .

Thus do they rove over Mackinac
Casting a spell of silent awe,
Folding their wings at the break of dawn—
Leaving the day to the snake and swan.

Chapel on Mount McKay

Lake Michigan

Discovery of the Five Great Lakes

THE Jesuits had become well acquainted with Lake Ontario, having paddled over these great lakes to the headwaters of the Ottawa. On Champlain's first visit he heard of a hidden water and a great sea. He was told that this hidden water lay between Lake Ontario and the Mer Douce. In sixteen hundred and thirty-four Jean Nicolet started from Three Rivers with two Jesuit Priests, called Father Breboeuf and Father Daniel, bound for the Huron country; they were hoping to found a Mission for the conversion of the red man. Seven Indians undertook to paddle Nicolet's canoes, and guide him along the intricate shore of the lake. They followed the same route that Father Le Caron had travelled twenty years before. They visited the Nipissings for a little while, and were friendly to Nicolet, and as he had heard terrible stories of them, he now knew they were misunderstood. At the mouth of French River, the Priests turned southward towards their chosen places, while Nicolet and his guides paddled in the opposite direction. They coursed the head of Georgian Bay, and paddled around the southern shore of the Manitoulin Island. Going through winding channels and beautiful islands they entered a broad strait, or river, which Etienne Brule had told them about. The current was strong, and they paddled through the most beautiful scenery. About twenty leagues they ascended the stream, when suddenly a long and dangerous rapids was before them. This has since been known as the "Sault Ste. Marie Rapids." The river was full of canoes and Indians fishing. Nicolet landed on the south shore and held a council with his Indians. This was the summer of sixteen hundred and thirty-four. Not speaking of the

Discovery of the Five Great Lakes

first visit of Brule apart from this, this was the first visit of the white man in Michigan soil. The Chippewas told Nicolet that he would have to carry his canoes around the Great Sault Rapids, and launch them above, and he would then reach the boundless water, a fresh sea water, and not the salt ocean that he was looking for. He wondered if the men of the fetid sea lived near, or if there was a people who had long hair; he had heard of this kind of people. There were also people who had neither hair nor beards, who smoked long pipes and looked like Frenchmen. The Ojibways could not tell him, but they said there was another people living on a lake to the south. Nicolet did not know whether these men were the people he was looking for or not, and the Indians could not help him. He asked them to give him guides, and never taking the trouble to look at the big sea he had been told about, he turned and retraced his steps down the broad river he had come up. And he went on until reaching the Lake of the Hurons, he again turned to the right and followed the shore on both sides of the main land. He was told that here was the passage way of the "Mer Douce," and entered a large lake to the west. He continued on, soon entering that great unknown sea since called "Lake Michigan." Ninety-nine years after Jacques Cartier discovered Mount Royal the Third Great Lake was discovered.

Discovery of the Five Great Lakes

Pie Island

Sault Ste. Marie, or Sault du Gaston

I proclaim and declare, at the door of this sea,
This spot is forever "The Sault Ste. Marie."

IN sixteen hundred and sixty-eight a small white settlement of twenty-five voyagers had been formed, and when Père Allouez came and sent back a glowing description of the promising condition of this Mission, the Superior of the Jesuits sent Father Père Jacques Marquette, and this great man left Montreal on April twenty-first, sixteen hundred and sixty-eight, to begin work at this Mission. The best blood of France flowed in his veins; for many generations his ancestors had been soldiers and statesmen, and gave their lives for the King. Marquette set sail in a little craft with a few others, and journeyed westward in birch-bark canoes. The red man and the white man bent to the paddle, and after many days reached their destination. Here Allouez met them, and a location was selected for the building of a station. First was erected a chapel, then a house was built for the Fathers, both for their own abode and for the entertainment of travellers. The ground about the tiny Post was ploughed and sown with wheat and

Discovery of the Five Great Lakes

peas and corn, in hopes the Indians would till the soil, but they held great aversion to the hoe. When it was finished, the whole was surrounded with a strong stockade of cedar twelve feet high as a means of protection; the whole occupied the point where in the American town Bingham Avenue and Water Street cross to-day, 1909. Here these men sought hardship, and truly found it; toil and famine and scarcity of all things, torment from the barbarians and mockery from the idolaters. It was at this time that Sault Ste. Marie took its final name. Here a vision of the Blessed Virgin came to Father Marquette, and the name was changed from Sault Du Gaston to Sault Ste. Marie. Up to this no religious Order save the Jesuits had come up the Great Lake district, but in 1670 Fathers Dollier and Galinee were fitted out by the Sulpicians of Montreal, and left with La Salle's expedition at midsummer of that year. When they came, they were treated kindly by Fathers Marquette and Dablon, but they did not want them. Three days they stayed, and departed back from whence they came.

The Peeping Squaw

Oh, Nanna, Nanna, is it true,
That you came up from the Sault,
And while sailing around the Cape,
You fell asleep just at the Gate,
And awakening full of rage and strife,
You banished your beloved wife,
That she should stand upon the "Pie,"
Where passing sailors hear her sigh;
And if the day is bright and fine,
She peeps to see if you are kind,
And if the weather is rough and raw,
You will not see "The Peeping Squaw?"

Grounds of Mr. King McVicar on McVicar's Creek

Discovery of the Five Great Lakes

Thunder Cape

'TIS the voice of the Giant who guards the Bay,
"Oh, white-winged ship make no delay,
For the war-birds of heaven are loose," he cries,
"I know their breath in the burning skies";
With folded arms, so mighty and strong,
The waves do his bidding and dash along;
But hark to the crashing, long and loud,
'Tis the chariot of God in the thundercloud.

Lake Superior

THE main features of Lake Superior are its size and its influence, because it is the largest of all bodies of fresh water. It is five hundred miles long, two hundred miles wide, and two thousand feet deep. It feeds the atmosphere in a wonderful way, and has long been spoken of as bottomless. The Indians call it the "Hidden Sea," and always have the idea that it has an underground sea, and when we look at the "Sault Rapids," it does not seem possible that so small a body of water can be the only outlet of Lake Superior. It is also known to have tidal waves, and that helps to place the theory of an underground sea. It may be that when the Indians called it a "Hidden Sea," that was their idea. It has a wonderful influence upon the atmosphere, absorbing the cold of winter, and in midsummer its coolness on these northern shores makes it a beautiful summer resort. It is grandly calm, and in its varied beauty and gloom in winter gives a new thought and charm to the eye, the different colors are so liquid and tinted in dark blues and greens. This great lake, with

Discovery of the Five Great Lakes

all the lesser lakes flowing into it, is well named Superior, and its waters are always cold as crystal. It has the greatest tonnage of any lake, and is making history from day to day. The Indians, when naming the district around about Lake Superior, called it "Algoma," meaning in the Indian dialect "Hidden." Henry Schoolcraft coined the word Algoma, making many dialect words from the Algonquin language. The meaning of the word "Algoma" is "Unknown," and is a coined word, such as Algic, and the word Algoma has been applied to this section of the country so long that few remember the beginning or what it means, but its real meaning is "Unknown," or "Hidden" country, an unknown land. When Louis Joliet came with his companion Père to explore the vast Hidden Sea, that was thought to be a salt water, and would bring them out to the shores of China, it was called "The Hidden Sea," and when Daniel Greysolon Duluth touched its shores for the first time, he embarked on the very spot that bears his name to-day, and in such great honor, he having taken the north shore of Lake Superior, and going farther west where Joliet gave his name. America certainly owes these men a deep debt, for this was the beginning of one of the greatest cities in the world. When the Jesuit Fathers and fur traders were hearing of a great sea hidden away, and century after century different countries had sent out knights who had been fired with the ambition to discover this great hidden sea, Jacques Cartier and Champlain and La Salle and hundreds of others went back disappointed. They thought this sea would bring them to China, and many were the wild ideas in the brains of these discoverers, but not until Joliet and the Jesuit Fathers came to the door of this great lake was it discovered.

Discovery of the Five Great Lakes The Indian Chiefs brought maps drawn with lines showing the outlets and inlets of this marvellous sea. Then when Jean Baptiste Talon, the Intendant of Canada, hurried to France and laid these discoveries at the feet of his King, he was thrilled with delight at the honor and glory he was bringing to France.

Nanna-Bijou's Blanket

The day was golden, and the age was new,
And the earth pace young when Nanna-Bijou
Canoed the Nepigon, calm and fair,
And found a mountainous barrier there.

In Indian rage and with might and main
He cut this mountainous ridge in twain,
And it shows to this day a monument to
The terrible rage of Nanna-Bijou.

He swam the Nepigon o'er and o'er,
And his blanket shows where it fell on the floor;
And there remains, where he dropped it down,
Though multiplied ages have come around.

The action of ages and ages unknown
Has turned this blanket to whitest stone;
But Indians trodding the snowy mat
Believe it the skin of the Rabbit Cat.

Nepigon River

Discovery of the Five Great Lakes

Silver Islet

Silver Islet

IN the early days they had no liquor at Silver Islet, but smugglers used to smuggle in the worst brands of whiskey ever drank by man. There was an old Scotchman who had considerable of this whiskey, and Capt. Frue had been watching him for a long time, but could not catch him. One day Capt. Frue sent for him and said: "Jock, if you will tell me where you get that whiskey I will give you a $5.00 bill." Old Jock stood thinking, then said: "Capt. Frue, I do not doubt your word, but I would like to have the $5.00 bill first." "All right," said Capt. Frue, and Jock started, taking Capt. Frue into the woods, coming upon a small trail where on one side of the trail was a big black stump. "Now," said Jock, "Capt. Frue, if you will put the $5.00 bill on the top of that black stump and walk on a bit, then turn and come back." The Captain did as he was told, and when he came back there stood a bottle of whiskey, but the $5.00 bill was gone and Capt. Frue was none the wiser.

Afterwards they opened a hotel and allowed each respectable man to have three drinks a day, but he could not treat his neighbor. Each man had a number on the blackboard and when a man went in to get a drink he drew a stroke on the blackboard, and when he got three he could get no more. It was only five cents a drink. That was on the Island; on the shore each man was allowed one bottle a week at fifty cents a bottle.

In the early seventies, when work was started at Silver Islet, Capt. Tewthrewy tells that a camp was made for making timber in the woods, and one day a wily old Ojibway Chief, named Blackstone, came with his followers and wanted something to eat. The cook put some lunch on the table and poured the tea in tin cups. This did not please the old Chief, he wanted cups and saucers. The cook would not give them to him. He was Scotch and had bright red hair. The old Chief came up and approached the cook and, putting his hands upon his head, said: "Oh, nice scalp!" "Oh, nice scalp!" The cook immediately brought him everything he wanted.

Discovery of the Five Great Lakes

※

Silver Islet Notes

WHEN the Silver Islet Mine gave out, the water was coming in at the rate of one hundred and fifty gallons a minute, and soon was drowned out.

The depth below the level of the lake was thirteen hundred feet.

There was said to be three hundred thousand dollars' worth of silver to be seen in the roof of the mine when flooded.

Everyone coming and going were supposed to be examined by the watchman, he making them take off their boots and coats while he ran his hands over them. They had a room for that purpose.

The greatest smugglers were women.

The John S. Tuttle, a steam barge loaded with coal from Buffalo, was held back by a storm and one hundred and fifty-six gallons a minute flooded the mine.

𝔇𝔦𝔰𝔠𝔬𝔳𝔢𝔯𝔶 𝔬𝔣 𝔱𝔥𝔢 𝔉𝔦𝔳𝔢 𝔊𝔯𝔢𝔞𝔱 𝔏𝔞𝔨𝔢𝔰

C. N. R. Elevator.   Largest in the World

𝔓ort 𝔄rthur and 𝔉ort 𝔚illiam

FORT WILLIAM was incorporated a town in 1892, but it has a history dating as far back as 1669. In that year the famous explorer, D. G. Du Lhut, built a trading post on the banks of the Kaministiquia. The French Government, in the year 1717, sent out an expedition to explore across the continent to the Pacific Ocean, with instructions to establish a post or base of supplies at what was then known as River Camistigoya, Lake Superior. A fort was erected on the present site of Fort William by Lieutenant Robertal de Lanone. From this date Fort Kaministiquia was used as a base of supplies for exploration and discovery. Here Verandrye and his gallant sons, in the year 1731, passed on to Rainy River and the "Great North-West." In 1782 the North-West Fur Co. had a post at Grand Portage moved, and established themselves on the Kaministiquia. The Fort was rebuilt in 1805, and named Fort William, which, together with Port Arthur, have reached a height that the wildest dreams of the prophecy of man could not have predicted. Lord Lorne poetically named it the Golden Gateway of the North-West, but it is the gateway no longer,

Discovery of the Five Great Lakes

it is the open door. It seems almost a fairy tale that in such a short time two such cities as Port Arthur and Fort William should stand at the head of Lake Superior, but it shows what the energy of man can do with natural resources at hand to help him. The future of these two cities is now assured. The Greater Fort William and Port Arthur is here and come to stay. The proud city of Port Arthur sits upon a hillside and does not hide her light under a bushel. Every cot and mansion contributes its share of welcome to the visitor who enters its gates. Fort William runs for miles, hidden by Mount McKay, with its miles of harbor for freighters and steamers, the largest on the lakes. In Port Arthur, on the terraced hill, are the proud homes of owners who have spared neither time nor money to adorn and beautify. The Emerson and McDougal and other lovely homes occupy commanding sites, while the Carrick, Brady and Walsh residences are situated near a murmuring brook which flows through the beautiful grounds, and these are only a few of the hundred of costly homes in the city of Port Arthur. Fort William is hidden behind Mount McKay from the sightseer who enters the harbor and bay, who is astonished at sight of the beautiful Italian villas and homes, of whose architecture any city would be proud. Fortunes have been settled and made in both Port Arthur and Fort William, making them indeed great cities on Lake Superior's shores, and those who come to see these prosperous cities do not see a landing place, but an open door, and are fascinated and stay. They have banking and commercial, milling, mining, coal handling, manufacturing, railway, grain handling and cleaning, and many other busy enterprises enjoying the swing of western life and bustle. Port Arthur and Fort William are connected by a line of electric street cars moving back and forth like a shuttle in

Discovery of the Five Great Lakes

a loom, weaving history as well as doing their part in the upbuilding of these great cities. These two cities are situated about one thousand miles from the Atlantic and nineteen hundred miles from the Pacific and five hundred miles from the shores of Hudson's Bay. The International Boundary is south of us sixty miles. Lake Superior is the largest body of fresh water in the world, and the beautiful harbor of Thunder Bay is second to none. The boats that touch at the docks can be counted by thousands and our shipments of grain would sound like a fairy story. These cities are the terminus for the Canadian Northern Railway and Northern Navigation Co., Booth and White Line Steamships and Canadian Pacific Steamships, with headquarters for the Canadian Northern Steamship Company. We are on the line of the Canadian Pacific Railway and soon will be connected with the Grand Trunk Pacific Railway.

To a Greater Port Arthur

Here's to the Landing, once the "Station,"
Entry place to a lusty nation—
Gate for His Majesty's legions, red,
Cheering the banner overhead.

Here's to Prince Arthur, it has been
Named for the son of our Queenly Queen,
Heart and heather are undefiled,
Royal, quite, as the royal child.

Here's to Port Arthur's open door,
Housing the wheat of the world—and more,
Taking the crop of the whole domain,
Sending it out to the world again.

Here's to a Greater Port Arthur, may
Time roll on till shall come the day—
Day of days—when the world knows she
Tallies the wealth of the Westland free.

Events Upon the Great Lakes

Discovery of the Five Great Lakes

THE Civil War created the demand for iron, and from this industry sprang the Soo Canal.

The Iron Mountain Road, when built from Marquette to the shores of Lake Superior, was the first road in the whole Northern country.

Mr. Ely built the first telegraph lines from Buffalo to Detroit, and from Pittsburgh to Cleveland. The demand for railroads made the demand for iron.

In 1887 the Mesaba Road opened up five roads: The Milwaukee, Geobic, Menominee, Wabash, and Minnesota.

This history of the world's three industries boomed the lakes.

The French brought the birch-bark canoe.

The first canoes the Jesuit Fathers found the Indians using were large enough to transport a family of five or six persons with all their luggage.

The merchants of Montreal went up to Fort William in a fleet of ninety canoes, which carried four tons burden and were paddled by eight or ten men. They were thirty feet long. These remained until the Nineteenth Century.

Furs were sent south by John Jacob Astor from Mackinac to the trading posts at Chicago.

After the loss of the "Griffon," a sixty-ton vessel, in 1679, sailing vessels did not appear on the lakes for seventy-five years.

The first steamboat made its appearance on the lakes in 1818, in the shape of a side-wheeler, naively called "Walk in the Water," and launched at Buffalo. An old painting shows her to be a little craft, with no pilot house, and a smokestack of six lengths of stove-pipe. She made money while she lasted, making all passengers pay eighteen dollars for a trip from Buffalo to

Discovery of the Five Great Lakes

Detroit. She had a monopoly for four years, and then one stormy night in October she went ashore after riding a terrible storm.

The first steamboat reached Chicago in 1832, and from that time they multiplied.

When copper ore began to be found it was necessary to have strong boats to carry it out.

For twenty years the people talked the Soo Canal. In 1855 Congress gave three million acres of land to aid the State of Michigan to build this Canal.

When the channel at Mackinac shows water inside of the ice navigation is open. Then ice-breakers thread their way through the floating ice with a string of vessels at their sterns. They are powerful craft, with a screw at the bow as well as at the stern. They first strike the water under the ice, so that the boat climbing upon it crushes it down, breaking it and throwing it out of the water, propelling the vessel through three or four feet of solid ice. This is an American invention, which is kept in their own waters.

The Detroit River has a record of a vessel every thirteen minutes of the day and night, averaging two hundred tons of freight a minute for the summer season.

Large shipbuilding yards are at Cleveland, and one of the largest is building this season in Port Arthur, making it one of the busiest seasons in all that country.

Since the toll of the "Griffon" and "Walk in the Water," every year thousands of tons freighters have been dashed to pieces, and the hair-breadth escapes are terrible.

It is the prophecy of the 20th Century that the Great Lakes will connect with the Atlantic by canal and river.

Vessels going direct from the ports of the Great Lakes to the old world, the development of the cities upon the borders of these Great Lakes is like a fairy story.

Discovery of the Five Great Lakes

Buffalo, Cleveland, Detroit, Milwaukee and Toledo are noted for their rapid growth. The people who dwell upon the shores of these Great Lakes give evidence of a wonderfully proud spirit and independent manner, and have a high enthusiasm for education.

The people seem to have an unrest for to work out the leadership of the cities, and strive for municipal and state conditions. Municipal importance is the watchword.

Chicago comes foremost as a city of great enthusiasm.

Henry Clay spoke in 1825 of the Soo Canal as these great waterways.

The cities and towns upon the borders of the Great Lakes may be proud, for to-day six of the cities have a population of nearly four million people, and are plainly seen to be the Gateway of the North.

In 1689 Count Frontenac was called to take the place of a Governor called Denonville, who had not been very successful. At this time England and France were at war. For the remaining nine years Count Frontenac devoted all his energies to defending New France against the English and Iroquois. In November, 1698, in his 78th year, he died and was deeply mourned as a strong Governor and beloved leader. He came out to New France in 1672, and during his long term of power and influence he built up settlements on the shores of the Great Lakes. He built a long line of trading posts. Five years before his death Frontenac had sent one of his men, Cadillac, to the Straits of Mackinac to hold that centre of the fur trade. Cadillac was a strong, forcible soldier, and well suited to the needs of the French fort. He had not gotten along well

Discovery of the Five Great Lakes

with the missionaries at Michillimackinac. They resented his presence and influence with the Indians. Cadillac saw that Detroit and Mackinac were the key to the interior. He hurried to Quebec to get ready for the fur trading on the Detroit River. He reached Detroit with a band of one hundred Indians on the twenty-fourth of July, 1701.

Through the Strait of Detroit more water flows than through any other river in the world. Through this channel, whose average width is a mile, and whose length is only twenty-seven miles, flow the waters of three lakes, Superior, Michigan, and Huron, with the hundreds of streams that feed them. This little river is the outlet for eight-two square miles of lake surface and one hundred and twenty-five square miles of land. Down this grand river floated beaver, mink and otter furs of immense value. It was the most beautiful spot in the world. From tree to vine squirrels bounded to collect apples and plums, which covered the earth. Quail, partridge and woodcock swarmed the woods. In the year 1702 the wife of Cadillac and Madame Donette came in open canoes. They were soon followed by the wives and families of other settlers. By 1708 the settlement had grown so fast that the houses of all outside of the stockade, twenty-nine huts, were not finished for the people. It was run first by the company, but after a time Cadillac got control, and ruled with as absolute sway as any feudal chief in his castle.

The importance of Niagara was early noticed by both the French and English, as well as the Iroquois. For twenty-five years the French and English applied to the Indian Councils for permission to build forts or trading-houses at that point, which no French diplomacy won. In 1720 Joncaire, with the help of Charles Le

Discovery of the Five Great Lakes

Moyne, gained from the Indians a reluctant consent, the request stipulating that the houses be of brick, for they knew the danger of stone forts, but the French kept on until they got the unwilling consent for the erection of stone houses, provided it be no stone fort. The French at once wrote to the King. The surrender of Niagara broke the line of connection with Montreal and the interior. In the year 1760 the Marquis of Vaudreuil signed articles of capitulation by which Canada and all its dependent posts had passed into the hands of the English, and French supremacy on the Great Lakes had ended. It only remained for the other French posts on the Great Lakes to be taken possession of.

Frontenac saw the importance of occupying strategic points on the lakes, and he himself went to Kingston. The fort bore his name, and he encouraged La Salle to build trading posts at Niagara, and did all in his power to gain Lake Erie and Ontario for the French. The French made their way seaward, and occupied the Strait of Detroit, and built forts at Sandusky. The French were travelling up the banks of lakes and rivers that brought them to the Mississippi by way of Chicago and Allouez to the southern country.

In the many struggles for possession of the Great Lakes, Mackinac and Sault Sainte Marie kept their possessions as trading and military forts.

By the middle of the Nineteenth Century Duluth was the most remote gateway of the Great Lakes, and had begun its history as a town.

The first attempt at mining was made in 1770 by Alexander Henry, the trader at Mackinac, after the Indian wars were over.

Copper and silver ore were the minerals that created most enthusiasm.

Port Arthur, Ont.

A view of Cumberland St., looking South

The City of Port Arthur gradually rises from the shores of Thunder Bay to a height of about 300 feet. It has broad, well-kept streets, substantial commercial buildings and a beautiful residential district laid out in terraces and lawns, from which there is an unsurpassed view of lake and mountain. This modern city is rapidly coming into prominence both as a manufacturing centre and a tourists' resort.

AS A MANUFACTURING CENTRE

on account of its geographical situation, at the head of navigation and the centre of Canada, with its exceptional transportation facilities, and waterfalls capable of generating over 145,000 h. p. assures cheap electrical energy.

AS A TOURISTS' RESORT

The following view of a camp in the vicinity of Port Arthur gives merely a suggestion of the pleasures awaiting for you in the life out of doors, of the days to be spent in the woods with their quiet and balm, on the streams and lakes in one's canoe either

fishing, hunting or exploring; and to suit the tastes of others, the city has golf links, tennis courts, beautiful winding roads, where you can, either on horseback or in automobile, find the recreation which all mankind needs to fit him to grasp the opportunities of life offered in our great and growing Dominion.

The Publicity Bureau, located at the intersection of the railway and steamboat lines, is ready at all times to furnish information to tourists and manufacturers.

An interesting book of information mailed on application to

N.G. NEILL, Industrial Commissioner, PORT ARTHUR, ONT.

ADVERTISEMENTS

George Hodder   Marion Merrill

The Algoma Hotel

NOT THE BIGGEST   BUT THE BEST

Strictly First-class   Rooms with Bath
Telephones in Rooms   Sample Rooms

The Algoma Buffet, the Finest Bar West of Toronto

Rates $2 to $5   American Plan

MERRILL & HODDER

PORT ARTHUR, ONT.   Props.

The Sleeping Giant of Thunder Bay slumbers still
BUT
Fort William, Ontario
The Young Giant of the Great Lakes

Pulsates through its LEFT hand with material prosperity of Western Canada while extending its RIGHT hand to Eastern Canada and the rest of the world. Fort William,

Fort William, Ontario, Victoria Avenue North

where Western Canada begins, holds out every economic and advantageous facility to manufacturers, wholesalers and warehousing for the great markets of Western Canada and export. Fort William has raw materials, cheap electric power and cheap coal; excellent water supply, clear, cold, soft, pure; splendid industrial sites with lake and rail facilities, and will grant reasonable concessions.

Full information promptly and with pleasure

HERBERT W. BAKER
Industrial Commissioner   Fort William, Ont.

ADVERTISEMENTS

Port Arthur, a jewel of price, set in a wheaten band of gold, the link between Mother East and Youthful, Progressive West, her leading Hardware establishment is worthy of her

WE CARRY the most complete and up-to-date retail stock in Canada to-day, being Jobbers and Importers of Shelf and Heavy Hardware; Cutlery, Domestic and Foreign; Lumbermen's and Contractors' Supplies. British Polished Plate Glass, Paints, Oils and Window Glass, Stoves and Tinware. Sporting Goods a Specialty. Hot Air, Steam and Hot Water estimates cheerfully submitted and installations made by experienced mechanics.

A TRIAL ORDER WILL BE APPRECIATED

WELLS & EMMERSON
PORT ARTHUR, ONT.

Grand Trunk Pacific Railway Elevator, Fort William, Ont. Largest Grain Elevator on Earth

THE JAMES WHELAN
Ice Breaker

From the first appearance of the James Whelan upon Lake Superior entering the harbors of Port Arthur and Fort William, she has become a citizen of the two cities. Mr. James Whelan has since arranged his great plant upon the banks of the Mission River. The James Whelan Ice Breaker and Wrecking Tug has entered into the hearts of the masters of the great fleets of steamers that used to hammer at the doors of our ice-locked harbor for days and weeks before her coming. On the first appearance of the tug some seasons ago she showed signs of such power and strength in her undertakings that, when she started out to help bring in a large fleet of vessels that were ice barred outside of Thunder Cape, she surprised the masters of the fleet, who were all unanimous in saying that the tug James Whelan was surely the best boat they ever saw working in ice. She has kept the harbor so that vessels coming up the lakes in the early spring had no fear of getting in, and the Great Dredging Company intend to keep up to date. Their large plant on Mission River is well equipped with everything that goes to make this company known all over the lakes. This spring the James Whelan has gone through ice from twenty-four to thirty-two inches in thickness, coming proudly in with a string of vessels behind her. On the coldest days she has made her way around the bay puffing proudly as she makes her way in. The Great Lakes Dredging Company have the first wireless installed upon the little Ice Breaker, showing that they are wide-awake to the needs of the harbors of Fort William and Port Arthur.

Port Arthur Insurance and Vessel Agency
GENERAL INSURANCE, LOANS AND SURETY BONDS
Limited

We represent the following Companies

Alliance Assurance Co.
Commercial Union Assurance Co.
Hartford Fire Insurance Co.
London & Lancashire Fire Insurance Co.
Manitoba Assurance Co.
New York Underwriters' Agency
Norwich Union Fire Insurance Society

Phoenix Assurance Co. of London
Royal Insurance Co., Limited
Rochester German Insurance Co.
Western Assurance Co.
London Guarantee & Accident Co.
Ocean Accident & Guarantee Co.
American Surety Co.

P. W. STURE, MANAGER   **PORT ARTHUR, ONTARIO**

Rutledge & Jackson
Are the Leading Men's Outfitters

A specialty of *Fine Tailoring* at moderate prices
Complete Lines of Women's Shoes—"*Queen Quality*"

LARGE STOCK OF MEN'S SLATER SHOES
We Dress Men from Head to Foot

Rutledge & Jackson
FORT WILLIAM   ONTARIO

The Red Cross Drug Store

is not as old as the

"SLEEPING GIANT"

but it has the progressiveness
that is born of youth.

This store makes a specialty of PURE DRUGS, PERFUMES, TOILET ARTICLES, etc. Tourists will always find here the CHOICEST BONBONS for ladies, and the best brands of IMPORTED and DOMESTIC CIGARS for gentlemen.

Remember the Sign of the Red Cross

A. L. SMITH, DISPENSING CHEMIST

PORT ARTHUR   ONTARIO

The Marks-Clavet-Dobie Co., Limited
PORT ARTHUR, ONT.

New Ontario's Largest Mercantile House

The
Marks-Clavet-Dobie Co.
Limited

IMPORTERS

Headquarters for Tourists' Supplies

FISHING TACKLE AND CAMP SUPPLIES OF EVERY DESCRIPTION

Our stock embraces Canoes, Tents, Camp Stoves, and everything used in a camp

We Make a Specialty of Outfitting Camping Parties

We gladly accord to tourists information as to fishing streams and the many points of interest in this locality, and the most direct way of reaching them

Sportsmen will find all their Requisites in our Establishment

ADVERTISEMENTS

The Molsons Bank

Incorporated by Act of Parliament, 1855

Capital authorized $5,000,000   Capital paid up $3,500,000

HEAD OFFICE . . MONTREAL

This bank has agents in the chief monetary centres the world over, and gives prompt attention to all banking business entrusted to it.

J. A. LITTLE, Manager Port Arthur Branch

T. N. ANDREW
FIRE INSURANCE

Money Advanced to Build Homes

ANDREW BUILDING
PORT ARTHUR, ONTARIO

J. T. STOCKS
DRUGS, TOILET ARTICLES PERFUMES, ETC.

J. T. Stocks   *Port Arthur, Ont.*

The Only Wholesale Grocery House
at the Head of the Lakes

THE RILEY-RAMSEY CO.
LIMITED

Wholesale Grocers and Importers

PORT ARTHUR   CANADA

The

Gaiety Theatre

A NEW AND UP-TO-DATE PLAYHOUSE
ON MODERN LINES

Vaudeville   Drama   Opera

The Gaiety Theatre

Cumberland St.   Port Arthur, Ont.

HEADQUARTERS
FOR

Port Arthur Views, Dainty Souvenirs, Pictorial Post Cards and Numerous Local Novelties

S. M. Lowery, The Bazaar, Cumberland St.

Stewart & Thompson

BOOKSELLERS
STATIONERS AND NEWSDEALERS

127 Simpson Street

FORT WILLIAM   ONTARIO

ADVERTISEMENTS

THE McFADDEN
MILLINERY EMPORIUM

Miss McFadden recognizes the value of fashionable and up-to-date millinery and gives a distinction and style to her hats, as she never duplicates her patrons' hats but gives to each a new individuality of its own. The Gage Hats and Ready-to-Wears, for tailored suits and wash dresses, are always to be found in the McFADDEN EMPORIUM.

SOUVENIR GOODS

Books, Picture Post Cards
Newspapers, Magazines
LARGE VARIETY

S. W. LOWRY, THE BAZAAR
32 Cumberland Street

Phone No. 470   56 Cumberland St.

W. T. McEACHERN

Manufacturing Chemist

PORT ARTHUR, ONT.

The Fallis-Tourtellot Co.

Wholesale and Retail Dealers in
HARDWARE

OUR SPECIALTY

Stoves, Tinware, Graniteware, Hardware for the Home

OUR MOTTO

Close Prices, Prompt Service in our Store and Quick Delivery

227 ARTHUR ST.   **PORT ARTHUR**

Docks and Yards, South Water St.
Telephones 15 and 85, P.O. Box 161

Louis Walsh Coal Co.

SHIPPERS AND DEALERS IN

ANTHRACITE, BITUMINOUS AND SMITHING COAL

Port Arthur   Ontario

ADVERTISEMENTS

TELEPHONE 301

Or Call and See Us when You Require
Any of the Following:

Electric Wiring	Telephones	Motors	Dynamos
Electric Signs	Lighting Fixtures		Reading Lamps
Shades	Tungsten Lamps		Electric Stoves

Automobile and Launch Supplies

PLUMBING AND HEATING

Repair Work in all Lines a Specialty

A. C. WALTZ & CO.   COURT STREET

Oscar Troostwyk

Accountant, Auditor and Assignee

P.O. BOX 224

PORT ARTHUR, ONTARIO, CANADA

The Big Store for Men

CLOTHING—Sole Agents for Semi-Ready

HATS—Agents for Christie, King and Stetson

BOOTS AND SHOES—Men's, Women's and Children's Shoes. Special Agents for Men's Regal Shoes. Dorothy Dodd Shoes for Women.

UNDERWEAR OF ALL KINDS   TRUNKS AND VALISES

Reliable Goods at Prices that Cannot be Duplicated

NIPISSING STORES, LIMITED

Cobalt   Port Arthur   Haileybury

Fortune's Ideal Clothing House

is just where the Ideal man can get fitted in Nobby Clothing, Shoes, Shirts, Ties and Collars

Cor. Pearl and Cumberland Streets
PORT ARTHUR, ONT.

Established 1878

A. McGILLIS
Clothier, Hatter and Furnisher
FOOTWEAR FOR ALL
PORT ARTHUR and FORT WILLIAM

DURING the past year we have built a new addition to our already large store, and have now over 28,600 square feet of floor area. This gives us additional purchasing power, and the success of all large stores depends on a large amount of business. In order to do this goods MUST and can be sold on a small margin. We therefore invite all those who contemplate furnishing homes to visit our

Carpet and House Furnishing and Furniture Departments on the Second and Third Floors

where we are showing the largest and choicest stock of goods in Northern Ontario. In our Ladies' "Ready-to-Wear" Department, we are showing some excellent values in Coats, Skirts and Costumes. Visit our new Dress Goods Department where everything is up-to-date and good value.

I. L. MATTHEWS & CO.
Dry Goods Importers   Port Arthur, Ont.

INTERESTING DRIVES

Aitken's Livery and Feed Stables

Carriages for all Functions and Competent Drivers When Desired

PLACES OF INTEREST IN VICINITY

Current River, three miles   Shuniah Mine, three miles
Fort William East, four miles   Dawson Road, twenty miles
    Kakabeka Falls, twenty-two miles
    Fort William West, seven miles
    Beaver Mine, twenty-five miles
    Badger Mine, twenty-six miles
    Silver Mountain, thirty-eight miles
    Silver Mountain, West End, thirty-nine miles
    Slate River Valley Mines, seventeen miles
    White Fish Lake, forty-one miles
    Mount McKay, seven miles from Port Arthur
    Pie Island (1150), twenty miles
    Thunder Cape (1350), sixteen miles
    Current River and Falls, three miles
    Nepigon River Famous Trout Stream, sixty-five miles
    Carp River Trout Fishing, sixteen miles
    McKenzie River Trout Fishing, fourteen miles
    Shooting Grounds
    Town Line between Oliver and Dawson Roads
    Old Rabbit Mountain Trail, Oliver Road
    Fort William Road to Murillo

ADVERTISEMENTS

Lyceum Theatre

Leading Vaudeville House of Port Arthur

MEMBERS OF LEADING AMERICAN AND CANADIAN THEATRICAL CIRCUITS

Lyceum Grill Room — *A Luxurious Restaurant in connection with the Theatre*

Phone 568   Estimates Furnished

J. G. KING, President   L. STANWORTH, Manager
H. A. McKIBBIN, Secretary

Stanworth, Martin Stone Company, Limited

Cut Stone and Monumental Contractors

ALL KINDS OF NATIVE AND FOREIGN MARBLES

PORT ARTHUR   ONTARIO

ADVERTISEMENTS

VIKERS, WALSH & CO.

Real Estate

FORT WILLIAM — ONTARIO

C. W. JARVIS   S. W. RAY

RAY, STREET & CO.
Established 1884

Bankers, Insurance, Real Estate

Port Arthur   Fort William

ELLIOTT & CO.

MANUFACTURERS OF

Mineral & Aerated Waters

PORT ARTHUR, ONT.

J. W. CROOKS & CO.
Port Arthur   Fort William

The Leading Drug Stores
OF NEW ONTARIO

EASTMAN KODAKS AND CAMERAS

Bank of Montreal

Established 1817

Capital, all paid up . $14,400,000.00
Rest 12,000,000.00
Undivided Profits . . 603,796.30

SAVINGS BANK DEPARTMENT

Interest allowed on deposits of $1.00 and upwards

Drafts Bought or Issued   Money Loaned

Sale Notes Collected and Forms Furnished
A General Banking Business Transacted

Port Arthur Branch   W. H. Nelson, Manager

IMPERIAL BANK

Head Office: TORONTO   OF CANADA   Established 1875

Capital Authorized . . $10,000,000.00
Capital Paid Up . . . 5,000,000.00
Reserve Fund . . . 5,000,000.00

A General Banking Business Transacted
Special Attention Given to Collections

SAVINGS DEPARTMENT

Interest Allowed on Deposits
from Date of Deposit

Port Arthur Branch: H. C. Houston, Manager

HEADQUARTERS FOR
SOUVENIRS

Native Agates   Chlorastrolites
Amethysts   Souvenir Spoons
Canadian Enamelled Jewelry

Port Arthur Jewelry Co.
PORT ARTHUR, ONT.

E. C. CURRIE CO.

Dry Goods   Ready-to-Wear
Millinery, Dress Making

E. C. CURRIE CO.

417-419 Victoria Ave.   Fort William, Ont.

Spence & Co.
PRESCRIPTION DRUGGISTS

Souvenirs, Post Cards, New Books, Magazines, Papers, Fancy Goods, Toilet Articles

304 Victoria Ave. and 1524 Edward Street
FORT WILLIAM, ONT.

HIGH-CLASS PORTRAITURE　　　　PICTURE FRAMING
VIEWS, GROUPS, ETC.　　　　　　ENLARGEMENTS

ROGERS' STUDIO
PORT ARTHUR
10 Cumberland St. North

PHONE 1125　　　　　　B. B. ROGERS, Manager

Pigeon Pine

IN WESTERN ONTARIO, on the banks of the Pigeon River, stand the magnificent forests of that timber which is now almost a thing of the past, known as the White Pine. Miles from any point at which it can be manufactured into lumber, and tributary to the Pigeon River, whose numerous rapids and high falls make driving a dangerous and costly proposition, these forests for years remained an example of the wonderful works of nature. About fifteen years ago these tracts of timber were acquired by the present owners, and after a large amount of money had been expended in improving the river, building dams, slides, and clearing the channel, the driving of these logs down the river was made possible. From the mouth of the Pigeon River these logs were towed to our large mills in Port Arthur, and there manufactured into different grades and sizes of lumber necessary to fill the orders of our numerous customers throughout entire Western Canada, where the users of good White Pine lumber appreciate the quality of our output.

With our large stock of about twenty million feet of lumber, we are able to supply, upon short notice, anything desired in lumber, lath and shingles.

The Pigeon River Lumber Co.

www.ingramcontent.com/pod-product-compliance
Lightning Source LLC
Chambersburg PA
CBHW071315060426
42444CB00036B/3046